DUNCAN MURPHY

Close Encounters Volume 2

Copyright © Duncan Murphy, 2018

All rights reserved. No part of this publication may be reproduced, stored or transmitted in any form or by any means, electronic, mechanical, photocopying, recording, scanning, or otherwise without written permission from the publisher. It is illegal to copy this book, post it to a website, or distribute it by any other means without permission.

First edition

This book was professionally typeset on Reedsy. Find out more at reedsy.com

Contents

Foreword	iv
THE CHARLES HICKSON & CALVIN PARKER ABDUCTION	1
THE LONGLEY ABDUCTION	13
THE LINDA CORTILE ABDUCTION	23
THE BETTY ANDREASSON ABDUCTION	34
THE KELLY CAHILL ENCOUNTER	45
Conclusion	56

Foreword

Congratulations on purchasing or borrowing *Close Encounters Volume 2: The Abduction Cases of Charles Hickson & Calvin Parker, Scott & Wendy Longley, Linda Cortile, Betty Andreasson, and Kelly Cahill* and thank you for doing so.

The following chapters will discuss five fascinating and thought-provoking alien abduction cases that are known to the public. We will examine the case of Charles Hickson & Calvin Parker, two co-workers who claim that peaceful a fishing trip in Mississippi became a horrifying ordeal when they were abducted by otherworldly beings. Next, we will look at the curious abduction case of the Longley family, that took place on a quiet stretch of road in Australia. Then we'll learn about Linda Cortile and her story of being taken from her Manhattan apartment, as well as the terrifying events that took place after her abduction. After that, we'll dive into the mysterious case of Betty Andreasson and how hypnotic regression brought forth memories of her being abducted multiple times by aliens over the course of many years. And finally, we'll investigate the Kelly Cahill incident, a terrifying tale involving a UFO, as well as dark mysterious beings with possible paranormal connections.

Whether you're a believer or a skeptic, these gripping true stories of Alien Abduction will give you much to ponder the next time you stare up into the starry night sky and find yourself asking, "Is there intelligent life somewhere up there among the stars?"

1

THE CHARLES HICKSON & CALVIN PARKER ABDUCTION

Charles Hickson and Calvin Parker were two friends and co-workers who found themselves caught up in an extraordinary tale that came to be known as the Pascagoula Abduction. The incident occurred in 1973, near Pascagoula, Mississippi and attracted a flurry of media attention.

In the wake of earlier incidents, such as the Betty and Barney Hill Abduction and the much-publicized and highly scrutinized Roswell Incident; the near frenzied level of public fascination in the Pascagoula Abduction would lead to much more general interest from the public on the topic of UFO's and Alien abduction.

A Night-Time Fishing Trip on the Pascagoula River

By all accounts, it was a cool, calm evening in Jackson, Mississippi, on the night of October the 11th, 1973. Two friends decided to go to the Pascagoula River to do a spot of night-time fishing. These two friends were 42-year-old Charles Hickson and 19-year-old Calvin Parker; both men worked together at the local shipyard and both men shared a keen interest in fishing.

The Pascagoula River offered some decent fishing during the evenings on the pier of the east bank where the men sat casting their lines out into the serene waters. The night promised to be a nice, relaxing one of leisure and quiet contentment. But unfortunately for the two fishermen, that was not to be the case.

Not long after dusk, Hickson was pleased to have gotten a nibble on his line and was beginning to reel it in, when he was interrupted by a strange and unnatural sound. The sound appeared suddenly and made both of the men feel inexplicably uncomfortable. The men have described this strange noise at various times since the night of the incident; They have described it as being a hissing sound, a whizzing sound, or a whirring sound.

The men looked around in an attempt to locate the source of what they were hearing. They were suddenly aware of flashing blue lights very close by. Hickson would later say that at first, he thought it was a police car flashing it's lights. But as the flashing lights began to approach the two men, they soon came to realize that the lights were attached to some kind of large, oval-shaped craft that was hovering some distance above the ground. Based on the description both men have separately given, it is believed by researchers that the craft was composed of some kind of unknown metal, and was a minimum of ten feet in height and upwards of forty feet in length.

When the mysterious craft reached the pier, it hovered over the two men. A few seconds later, a door opened and the entire pier was bathed in a bright light that emanated from within the doorway of the craft. Shielding their eyes from the bright light, the two men squinted to see three grey humanoid beings floating out of the hovering craft and descending down toward them.

As described by the two witnesses, the movement of these strange beings gave an impression almost as though they were somehow robotic or mechanical in nature. Charles Hickson later described some of the details of the beings physical appearance. He said that they were humanoid in shape, but according to his description, they didn't have necks. Additionally, he said that they had a very thick, coarse skin and he described it as being wrinkled like the skin of an elephant's trunk. According to Hickson, their skin was so thick and wrinkled that he couldn't make out whether or not the beings had eyes. The creatures were also said to appear to possess small slits for mouths.

Hickson also later recalled that each of these strange beings had some sort of projections coming out of the sides of their heads in place of ears and noses, and these projections were similar in size and shape to carrots. He also described that the beings hands were like claws, and were gloved in some kind of mittens. Furthermore, while they did seem to have legs, they were joined together, something similar to a pedestal with a single elephant-like foot at the end; and rather than walking, the creatures glided above the ground.

Although the two men were completely conscious and fully aware, they describe themselves as being in a state of paralysis wherein they were unable to move or do anything. Hickson later recalled that he didn't know whether he was simply paralyzed by fear, or whether the floating creatures had somehow done something to take away their ability to move.

The two paralyzed men were then levitated off the ground — or "floated", as they later described the experience — and brought aboard the massive, metallic hovering craft.

Abduction and Examination

Once on board the craft, the men both reported feeling physically numb and both remained paralyzed. The younger man, Calvin Parker, claimed that he had lost consciousness for at least part of the ordeal on account of the fright caused to him by the experience.

Hickson however, later recalled his time aboard the alien vessel in startling and unsettling detail. As Calvin Parker was unconscious at the time, we only have Charles Hickson's word to go on from at this point. Hickson described the scene aboard the craft as unfolding in a relatively short amount of time. The men were separated into different parts of the ship. Hickson claimed that the beings continued to levitate him into an 'operating theatre', there he floated stationary in the air as though resting on an invisible table. According to Charles Hickson, whilst he remained paralyzed and numb to sensation, he did retain use and movement of his eyes and was thus able to get a relatively good look at what was transpiring around him.

Mr Hickson found himself surrounded by the strange alien beings and he observed an object levitate over and around his body. He described this object as having a metallic exterior with a large aperture in the shape of a football that appeared to Hickson to be some sort of mechanical eye. The device hovered over him and moved up and down his body, in what seemed to

Hickson to be some sort of examination scan or a "probe" as he later called it.

At this point in the abduction account, the alien creatures along with their mechanical probe, suddenly left the room that Charles Hickson was being held in, presumably as Mr Hickson supposed, to perform the same procedure on Calvin Parker. Mr. Parker, had no immediate memory of the events that took place aboard the alien craft, although whether his lack of memories where the result of being unconscious or if his memories of the ordeal were repressed through some other means was not clear until sometime later.

The next thing that Hickson could recall was being levitated, or in his words "floated" back down from the alien vessel, back onto the pier. He said that he could feel his feet dragging as he was levitated, still paralyzed and motionless, back down onto the ground. Calvin Parker was also levitated back down to their original position on the riverbank alongside Mr. Hickson.

The men estimated, with Charles Hickson providing most of the details to base their estimation on, that the whole encounter had lasted no more than approximately twenty minutes; from initially hearing the strange sound, to being placed back down on the pier.

Contacting the Authorities

Immediately after the incident, Charles Hickson and Calvin Parker were understandably stunned and terrified by their experience. Both men claimed that they got into their car and just sat there in silence for at least forty-five minutes. Hickson admitted to drinking some whiskey at this time to help calm his nerves.

Skeptics often point out Charles Hickson's consumption of whiskey in an attempt to call into question the legitimacy of the men's story. While alcohol certainly would dull the senses and limit one's mental capacities, it must be noted that, as per the recounted recollections of both men, the alcohol consumption only came after the encounter with the alien creatures had already taken place, and it was only Charles Hickson, and not Calvin Parker, who took part in the alcohol consumption.

In any event, after the men were able to adequately calm themselves, the next step for them was to try to decide what to do next. They discussed their options. Both men felt reluctant to share the account of their ordeal, as neither of the men wanted any attention regarding the incident; They certainly didn't want the media to get a hold of the story, out of fear that the strange and unbelievable nature of the story would lead to an intense level of public scrutiny, ridicule and potential invasion of privacy.

However, despite their reprehension of sharing the account of their ordeal, the men where both firmly in agreement that the incident was a matter of national security and as such, it needed to be immediately reported to the authorities. After some debate as to who they should report the incident to, they decided that their best option was a military one, as whatever they had just witnessed was clearly beyond the purview of local law enforcement. So they made contact with the Keesler Air Force Base; an Air Force base that operated close to the nearby city of Biloxi, Mississippi.

Seeing as the UFO that Hickson and Parker encountered seemed to be some kind of aircraft, despite levitating without the use of traditional propulsion methods such as a propeller, a rotor or jet engines, it stood to reason that the most qualified authority to address the situation would have been the United States Air Force. The 1970s were firmly in the 'popular UFO era', and it was already publicly speculated that the Air Force was or had been investigating sightings and encounters with unidentified flying objects. Not to mention the fact, that this strange event occurred during the height of the Cold War; It was a time of extremely heightened tensions, in which the United States Military was looking for any potential edge over their communist enemies.

Having taken all these things into consideration, Charles Hickson and Calvin Parker contacted officials at the Keesler Air Force Base and were met with a surprising response. They were told by Air Force personnel that, "The United States Air Force does not deal with that sort of thing. We don't investigate UFOs".

Naturally, this response by Keesler Air Force Base raises a few questions. Why did these Air Force officials deny Charles Hickson and Calvin Parker? Were the Air Force personnel simply skeptical of the credibility of the two men, or were there other factors at play? Even if the men were just making up a false story, wouldn't it behoof the United States Air Force to investigate any and all claims of advanced, unidentified aerial craft? If the United States Air Force's core mission is to maintain American air superiority, wouldn't they want to look into any and all claims of superior aircraft operating within US air space? For all the Air Force personnel knew, the UFO that Hickson and Parker had encountered could have been some kind of experimental secret Soviet aircraft. The more we consider the questions, the less sense the scenario makes.

It should be noted, of course, that Project Blue Book, the famous study to systematically investigate UFOs and the UFO phenomenon that was conducted by the United States Air Force, had been terminated just four years earlier. So while what the Air Force told Hickson and Parker was technically true, one nevertheless struggles to comprehend how and why Keesler Air Force base considered an alleged encounter with an unknown technologically advanced air craft operating within their air space to not be within their jurisdiction.

Regardless, Charles Hickson and Calvin Parker were turned away by the United States Air Force, and so with nowhere else to turn, they went to the only other place they could think of: the Jackson County Sheriff's Office.

It was about 10:30 PM when the two men arrived at the sheriff's office. They brought with them, a pair of catfish they had caught during the evening's fishing trip prior to encountering the UFO, as the fish were all they had to back up that their story. The sheriff of Jackson County at the time was a man by the name of Fred Diamond. Sheriff Diamond listened to the two witnesses tell their story. He was receptive of the story, and according to his own comments on the incident, he felt that the men appeared to be both sincere and truly frightened. The sheriff also noted that he felt that Calvin Parker seemed particularly disturbed by what had transpired.

However, Sheriff Diamond was nevertheless skeptical of the story he was told by Hickson and Parker. Which is understandable, who wouldn't be skeptical of a couple of seemingly eccentric men suddenly showing up at the police station unannounced, to tell a fantastical tale of alien abduction, whilst carrying a pair of catfish and smelling heavily of whisky? The sheriff was understandably reluctant to fully support the men's story.

The Secret Tape

In order to get to the bottom of this strange and bizarre tale, Sheriff Fred Diamond decided to interrogate Charles Hickson and Calvin Parker. He brought the two witnesses into an interrogation room and got them to run through the story for him. After relating the story to the sheriff again, the sheriff asked them repeated questions, trying to trip them up through cross examination. Despite the Sheriff's intense questioning, Hickson and Parker's story remained entirely consistent.

After a line of tough questioning, the sheriff executed a master stroke in his plan to catch out any dishonesty in Hickson and Parker. He left the room, leaving Charles Hickson and Calvin Parker alone to talk among themselves. Unbeknownst to Hickson and Parker, Sheriff Diamond also left a hidden microphone in the interrogation room and secretly recorded the two rattled men's conversation. Certainly, any false information or fabricated elements of the story would come to light when the two men were given an opportunity to talk in what they thought to be privacy.

And the men did talk, but there were no efforts to get any stories straight, no ironing out of small details, no aligning of timelines or collaborating on the unfolding of events. No, instead, the microphone recorded two deeply disturbed men, struggling to comprehend the surreal and horrific evening that they had just experienced.

The tape of the interview itself and the included audio conversation between the two men when they were alone continued to be held on file for many decades at the Jackson County Sheriff's department. The tape has also been copied and circulated widely among UFO investigators and enthusiasts, and it can still be tracked down to this day.

By the following day after the night of strange encounter, the local media had somehow managed to get hold of the story and contacted Sheriff Diamond at the sheriff's office for comment. When Charles Hickson and Calvin Parker went into work the following day, they chose not to discuss the abduction incident, however, their work colleagues began to notice that the pair, especially Calvin Parker, were particularly agitated and on edge. By the time Sheriff Diamond called their workplace to let them know about the media attention, it was too late, the story had spread, and soon would be picked up by media outlets around the world.

Eventually, the men both moved to the neighboring county, having grown tired of the unwanted media attention.

Although both men have taken and passed numerous polygraph tests to confirm that they both, at very least, believed their story of the incident to be true as they remembered it, they never were able to avoid doubtful scrutiny from skeptics or ridicule from the media.

Charles Hickson died in September 2011, at age 80. He maintained the truth of his story until his death. Calvin Parker is said to have fared quite poorly mentally and emotionally from the ordeal and has long since retreated from the public eye.

*The following text is a partial transcript of conversation that took place between Charles Hickson and Calvin Parker. It is from the Jackson County Sheriff's Office secret tape recording.

CALVIN: I got to get home and get to bed or get some nerve pills or see the doctor or something. I can't stand it. I'm about to go half crazy.

CHARLES: I tell you, when we're through, I'll get you something to settle you down, so you can get some damn sleep.

CALVIN: I can't sleep yet like it is. I'm just damn near crazy.

CHARLES: Well, Calvin, when they brought you out-when they brought me out of that thing, goddamn it! I like to never in hell got you straightened out.

CALVIN (Voice raised): My damn arms! My arms! I remember they just froze up and I couldn't move. Just like I stepped on a damn rattlesnake.

CHARLES: They didn't do me that way.

CALVIN: I passed out. I expect I never passed out in my whole life.

CHARLES: I've never seen nothin' like that before in my life. You can't make people believe-

CALVIN: I don't want to keep sittin' here. I want to see a doctor-

CHARLES: They better wake up and start believin'... they better start believin'.

CALVIN: You see how that damn door come right up?

CHARLES: I don't know how it opened, son. I don't know.

CALVIN: It just laid up and just like that, those son' bitches-just like that, they come out.

CHARLES: I know. You can't believe it. You can't make people believe it-

CALVIN: I paralyzed right then. I couldn't move-

CHARLES: They won't believe it. They gonna believe it one of these days. Might be too late. I knew all along there was people from other worlds up there. I knew all along. I never thought it would happen to me.

CALVIN: You know yourself I don't drink.

CHARLES: I know that, son. When I get to the house, I'm gonna get me another drink. Make me sleep. Look, what we sittin' around for? I gotta go tell Blanche... what we waitin' for?

CALVIN (panicky): I gotta go to the house. I'm gettin' sick. I gotta get out of here.

Sound of Charles getting out of his seat and leaving the room.

CALVIN: It's hard to believe . . . Oh God, it's awful... I know there's a God up there...

2

THE LONGLEY ABDUCTION

On the evening of Saturday, March the 16th, 1996, the Longley family were traveling in their car to their hometown of Grafton in New South Wales, Australia, from the town of Lismore, where they had been on a day trip to visit friends of the family.

Scott Longley was driving the vehicle, while his wife Wendy Longley, rode in the passenger seat. Their two children, two-and-a-half-year-old Scott Jr, and one-and-a-half-year-old Bronwyn occupied the back seat of the vehicle.

The Longley family had wrapped up their visit with their friends in Lismore, said their goodbyes and left for home sometime early in the evening, approximately 7 pm. The family made a short stop at a Hungry Jack's fast food restaurant (Australia's version of Burger King), got some takeout food from the drive thru, and continued on their way back home to Grafton. So far, a lovely, wholesome day with nothing strange or unusual to report. But that was about to change for the Longley family.

On a dark, unlit section of open road, about five miles north of the town of Casino, Scott Longley noticed two unusual lights appear in his rear view mirror. Scott had not seen any other cars on the road for quite some time, so he had taken particular notice of the strange lights. He returned his eyes to the stretch of road ahead of him, dismissing the lights behind as an approaching car or something similar. But when he glanced in the rear view mirror again, the strange lights had begun to change. Scott described them as being yellow in color and surrounded by something like a halo of white light.

Scott Longley again returned his gaze to the road ahead of him, trying to maintain his focus and not be distracted by anything, yet his eyes couldn't seem to resist being drawn to the lights in the rear view mirror.

The next time Scott looked back in the rear view mirror, the two yellow lights began to move inward to one other, and gradually merged into one single bright light. While Scott was intrigued and somewhat mystified by the lights he was seeing, he made the decision to not say anything about them to his wife out of fear of potentially frightening her. However, regardless of Mr. Longley's choice not report what he was seeing to his wife, she certainly hadn't been spared the potential fright of seeing unusual lights in the night.

As Scott Longley was fixated by the lights in his rear view mirror, Wendy Longley's attention was drawn to an even more brilliant display of unexpected lights. According to the witness, as little as one-hundred feet away from the passenger side of the vehicle, a whole myriad of floating lights were dancing in the darkness.

It was estimated by the witness that somewhere in the vicinity of two-hundred or more strange lights, or 'fairy lights' as she described them, danced around in the near distance. She described some as being pure white lights, while others appeared to be a bright pale green color. Wendy observed these lights for only a few seconds before losing sight of them. She then asked her husband if he had seen the lights that she had been looking at. He replied that he had not seen those lights but had in fact been watching lights very similar to what she was describing in the rear view mirror.

They discussed the unusual sighting for the rest of the drive home, but as far as they could immediately tell, there was nothing else strange or out of the ordinary with the experience.

Back Home

The Longley family arrived back at their home in the city of Grafton at around 9:30 pm. Wendy noted that she felt that the journey home seemed to have taken longer than it usual did. It was the couple's custom to retire to bed generally at around 10:30 pm, however, despite it having been a long and tiring day, they both ended up staying up later than they usually would have. Wendy didn't go to bed until around midnight, while Scott stayed awake watching TV until around 2:30 am. They both claim that they felt unusually active and energetic that evening.

The following morning, Sunday the 17th of March, Scott awoke at 5 am and went for a run with a running partner. Scott was a very experienced runner, having kept up the practice for some twenty-five years. As he began his morning run, he noticed a momentary pricking sensation in his left nostril that disappeared almost immediately. About halfway into his run, he began to develop a painful blister on the big toe of his right foot. In all of his years of running, this was the first time he had ever developed a blister. It became too uncomfortable to continue running, so Scott returned home. On the walk home, he began to develop cold-like symptoms, including a runny nose, something highly unusual for Mr. Longley.

When he arrived back home, he discovered that his entire family were also experiencing cold-like symptoms. Wendy had a sore throat, and she was experiencing severe discomfort in her left ovary. Scott Jr had an excessively runny nose, and disturbingly, there were signs of blood in his mucous.

Prior to this, Scott Jr had only ever come down with one cold, and he had never ever experienced any previous nose-bleeds at all. Normally, the toddler was a good sleeper, reliably sleeping through most nights undisturbed. After the night of March 16th however, Scott Jr didn't sleep well for the following two weeks.

The Monday following the event, the 18th of March, Wendy contacted a UFO research group located in Sydney by telephone, as by this point, they had begun to look into unconventional explanations for what they were experiencing, having come up short trying to explain their experience via conventional means. Wendy was put in contact with UFO researcher Moira McGhee, who would prove to be very helpful for the Longleys. In the course of the conversation with Moira, Wendy was asked about potential lost time, and the researcher suggested that perhaps hypnotherapy could be useful for both Wendy and Scott.

On the following Wednesday, the 20th of March, the local newspaper published an article featuring a local UFO researcher by the name of Gary White. Mr. White was seeking assistance in locating potential witnesses who may have seen a UFO in the area the previous Saturday night.

Wendy did not hesitate to contact Mr. White, who was highly

responsive and set up a meeting right away. During the meeting with Gary White, Scott and Wendy told Mr. White about the lights that they had seen and the circumstances surrounding the event. They also told him about the subsequent cold-like and otherwise unusual symptoms that the family had experienced in the days after their encounter with the strange lights. Mr. White took some photographs of Scott's blister, and he also took photographs of a pair of red marks that Mr. White had noticed on the back of both Scott and Wendy's necks.

Wendy brought up the idea of hypnotherapy with Gary White, and he agreed that it could indeed be very useful. The Longley's made contact with a hypnotherapist, a woman known only to researchers as 'Sue', and arranged for a series of hypnotic regression sessions. The first of these sessions was to take place approximately two weeks later.

Hypnotic Regression Therapy

Scott was the first to undergo hypnotic regression therapy. In total, he would participate in three of such regression sessions. Wendy's retrieved memories from her regression session were admittedly blurred and vague, but they corroborated many key details that would be revealed in her husband's regressions.

Under regression, Scott recalled in great detail, events that he didn't even know had happened in the first place. Under hypnotic regression, Scott described an out-of-body experience. He was able to see into the family car from a bird's eye point of view; it was as though he were above the vehicle, looking down at it from some height up in the air. He could see that the vehicle was not moving and had come to a complete halt on the road.

He could see himself sitting in the driver's seat, while his wife sat in the passenger seat asleep and still. He could see both of his children as well. Bronwyn was also fast asleep, belted into her child seat. Scott Jr was also in the rear of the vehicle sitting next his sister in his own child seat, although he appeared to be awake and attentive.

Scott then saw two beings approach the vehicle. He called them aliens, and described them as being quite tall, approximately 210 cm by his estimation, and that their skin was a greyish color, like that of smoke or ash. He also described the beings as having small ears, and large black eyes. Additionally, he described them as having small mouths without lips and two small dots in place of noses.

He said that he was able to observe the alien beings from this bizarre, out-of-body perspective, as they approached the driver's side door of the family car. The alien creatures opened the driver's side door, and the hypnotically regressed Scott Longley saw them unbuckle his seatbelt and remove him from the vehicle. According to Mr. Longley, the two beings carefully removed him from the vehicle and held him outside of it for some time.

Meanwhile, two more alien beings, of the same physical description as the first two, approached the other side of the vehicle. They opened the passenger side door and removed Wendy Longley from the car in the same manner the first beings had removed Scott.

Scott described seeing another alien being approach the vehicle, this alien was of a smaller stature than the others. This small being opened one of the rear doors of the car and attempted to disengage the safety belt of Bronwyn's child seat. This smaller being was unsuccessful however, and it was soon joined by a second small alien being and together these two small aliens were able to gently remove the toddler from the vehicle. Together with two of the larger alien beings, the beings took Scott's wife Wendy and Scott's infant daughter Bronwyn into a field off to the side of the road. At this point, the Scott's son, Scott Jr, was still inside the car.

Scott claims that he then witnessed the alien beings carry himself around to the back of the family car, where they placed him face down on the ground. One of the beings carefully held Scott's head up off the ground. Still observing the scene from somewhere up above, Scott then witnessed the beings use a device, that he described as looking somewhat reminiscent of a silver staple gun, to press something into the back of his neck.

He also said that he witnessed the creatures perform some kind of procedure that seemingly involved them inserting something into the big toe of his right foot.

At this point, Scott Longley said that the beings turned him over onto his back, lifted up his shirt and began to examine his abdomen. Scott had been in a car accident the previous year, and as a result had sustained a stomach injury and now had a prominent scar. According to Mr. Longley, the alien beings seemed particularly interested in that scar.

At this juncture, the hypnotically regressed Scott Longley observed from above, the Scott Longley on the ground stand up, at which time, the viewpoint of the observing Scott Longley merged with that of the one below, and the hypnotically regressed Scott Longley was now recalling the scene in the first person. Most bizarrely of all, Scott found that he was now able to communicate telepathically with the alien beings, and he proceeded to ask them what they wanted with his family.

Scott asked the alien creatures what their purpose was. They told him that they were a lost family, and they gave a telepathic impression that they wanted to obtain a sample from Mr. Longley. They told him that they could see that Scott and his family were happy and encouraged him to continue living a happy life and being kind to others. Scott said that at this point, he saw that his son, Scott Jr, was out of the car. The boy was running around and playing with the smaller aliens that were around the same size as the boy. Scott got the impression these smaller alien beings were around the same age as his son. His son was laughing as he played with the aliens, and Scott felt that the alien beings were laughing with him. They also seemed to be communicating with each other, the creatures along with the young toddler.

Scott later said that he sensed no danger and he felt no fear. He felt completely comfortable being in the alien beings presence, and he felt comfortable with them interacting with his family. He recalled thinking that the alien creatures were a beautiful and kind people. At this point, Scott noticed that the alien beings were carrying his wife and daughter back to the family car. The beings placed them back into their respective seats within the vehicle and re-fastened their safety belts. He even said that it appeared as though one of the alien beings even leaned in and kissed his wife on the cheek.

Scott claims that he then saw a small crowd of the alien beings in the field where his son had been playing with the smaller creatures. He said that there were at least twenty alien beings in this small crowd that had gathered in the field. He then saw a vessel that he described as a spacecraft, hovering above him. The aliens telepathically communicated to Scott that they 'wanted him'. Scott protested, communicating to the beings that he could not go with them, as he needed to remain with his wife and children.

Scott claims that he then noticed that the crowd of alien beings seemed to suddenly vanish. In the blink of an eye, he was alone. But no sooner could he attempt to take stock of his situation, he suddenly found himself on top of a table, in a completely different place altogether. It was as though he had been inexplicably teleported to this new location. There were alien beings with him again, however, this time they were now a different type of alien creature. (Unfortunately, Scott Longley did not provide a description as to how these new alien beings were different from those that he had encountered by the family car)

Scott recalled being strapped down to a table. He described the table as being longer than he was tall, with Mr. Longley stating that his own height is approximately 175 cm. By Scott's estimation, the table was somewhere between 6 cm and 8 cm in thickness. He described an array of very bright lights that was above him and to his left, and he also said that there were three round lights directly above his position. He also said that he noticed some kind of arm, perhaps mechanical in nature, which was affixed to one end of the table, at the end of this arm were four appendages that Mr. Longley described as 'claws'.

And then just as suddenly as he arrived on that bizarre table, he was back in the family car; Back on the road between Lismore and Grafton, a few miles north of Casino. He said that he put a hand on his wife's knee, and then both his wife and his daughter awoke from their slumber.

Back Home Safely

The rest of the evening of March 16th played out under hypnotic regression exactly as it had in the initial memories of Scott and Wendy Longley. It seemed that Scott Jr had remained awake during the entire event, but being that he was barely older than an infant, if he did remember anything from the bizarre and highly mysterious event, he certainly wasn't able to communicate his experiences.

One more curious thing was revealed under Scott's hypnotic regression. Later that night when they arrived back at their Grafton family home, long after the children had been put to bed and also after Wendy had finally gone to sleep much later than usual, Scott looked out of a window and, only under regression, he recalled seeing the spacecraft hovering in their back yard. He telepathically asked what they were doing there, and he got back a telepathic response. The alien beings told him that they just wanted to make sure that the Longley family had gotten home safely.

3

THE LINDA CORTILE ABDUCTION

The popular imagery of alien abduction has become so pervasive that just about everyone will have some kind of image come to mind when the topic comes up in conversation. Likely that mental image is of some kind of flying saucer, hovering in the sky, with a single beam of white light shining down from it, illuminating a farmer's field, or a deserted stretch of highway, or some rural outpost surrounded by miles of desert.

If that imagery seems familiar, it could be for a couple of reasons. It could be because these are the types of alien abduction images that have entered the public consciousness as a result of 20th century popular culture. Or it could be that if aliens are going to come down from outer space to abduct humans off the face of the Earth, and want to do so in a covert, surreptitious manner; then it would stand to reason that some quiet, secluded place would be the ideal location to pick someone up without drawing any undue attention.

'Alien abduction is something that only occurs in remote rural backwater places and other than the abductees themselves, there are never any reliable witnesses to the event.' This is what seventy-plus years of stories since the beginning of the modern UFO phenomenon in popular culture has taught us to expect. And that's also what makes the story of the abduction of Linda Cortile so interesting: it happened in Manhattan, New York, one of the most densely populated places in the world; with multiple eyewitnesses to the abduction.

Abduction in Manhattan

In the early morning hours of November the 30th, 1989, Linda Cortile was peacefully sleeping in her bed, in her 12th story New York apartment. Her apartment was located on the lower east side of Manhattan, just across from the Famous Brooklyn Bridge.

Linda awoke at around 3 am that morning. At the foot of her bed, she was startled to see a number of figures standing and watching her intently. She was aware that her doors and windows had all been closed and locked, so nobody should have been able to enter her apartment uninvited; at least not without making enough noise to wake both Linda and her husband from their slumber.

In her drowsy and disoriented state, the next thing Linda knew, she was suddenly somewhere else, laying on some kind of medical examination table. There were several of the unusual figures from her bedroom surrounding the table where she lay motionless. Then suddenly, she found herself back in her bed within her apartment again, and the strange beings that had been standing by the foot of her bed were gone. Her memories were extremely fragmented and her husband remained asleep beside her, just as if nothing had happened at all.

Earlier that year, Linda had read a book called *'Intruders: The Incredible Visitations of Copley Woods'*. It was written by a man who was quite likely the most highly respected and renowned UFO researcher in the field at the time, Budd Hopkins. Being familiar with Mr. Hopkins' work and knowing that he would not only be likely to believe her story, but could quite possibly also provide her support and assistance, given his reputation for doing the same for others who had been contacted by aliens, Linda decided to contact Budd.

Budd Hopkins had spent a lifetime investigating UFOs and had already written two books on the topic of alien abduction by the time of Linda Cortile's abduction (it was the second of these two books that Linda had read earlier that year). Rather than simply dealing with dry clinical reports of close encounters and UFO sightings, Budd Hopkins developed a reputation for working closely with abductees who had had firsthand experience with alien beings. He cared deeply for the physical and emotional well-being of the subjects of his investigations. He was tireless in his efforts to get people recognition for their close encounter experiences and also get them the help and support he so felt they needed and deserved. It was because of this tireless crusading and investigating that Budd earned the title, 'The Father of the Abduction Movement'.

After speaking with Budd Hopkins and discussing her experience with him, he suggested that Linda try undergoing hypnotic regression therapy. She agreed and underwent the hypnotic procedure soon after.

As a result of Linda's hypnotic regression therapy, she was able to recall the events of the night of November the 30th, 1989, with a great deal of added detail.

She recalled waking up that night and seeing five beings in

her bedroom. But just as she had previously recalled, all of the windows and doors in the apartment had been locked, so it wasn't immediately clear how the beings had entered her apartment. With these beings standing all around her bed, she began to levitate out of bed and up into the air.

Linda's body floated upward until she was about to reach the ceiling. But instead of simply bumping into the ceiling and stopping, her body continued to rise and she passed right through the ceiling, as though it wasn't there. The alien beings levitated her in an upright standing position. In her words, "It was as though I was standing on nothing but air."

Linda found herself floating through the open air over the Manhattan skyline with three of the five alien beings floating by her side. She described seeing a flying disc above her in the sky, which she understood to be the alien beings spacecraft. After Linda and the alien beings had boarded the disc shaped craft, she remembered that inside, she saw of a lot of benches and doors that she described as sliding open as she was escorted down a hallway by the beings.

Everywhere that she could see, Linda described seeing buttons and lights that were very prominently on display all around her. She told Budd Hopkins, that after being taken deep inside the alien craft, the alien beings laid her down and secured her to a large slab table.

At this point, Linda felt fear rising up in her chest. She recounted that she screamed and yelled, but the beings didn't seem to be bothered by her distress. Finally, after a period of incessant yelling and screaming, one of the beings approached her and said something in a language that she didn't understand. The being then covered her mouth with one of it's hands and prevented her from screaming until their procedure was complete.

Unexpected Witnesses

In the days and weeks after Linda's experience, the case began to get some media attention. Mostly, this public exposure served only to make Linda's life much more difficult and destroyed all sense of her personal privacy. But before long, there was an unexpected break in the case.

Budd Hopkins received a communication from two men who claimed that they had witnessed Linda's abduction. The two witnesses identified themselves only as "Dan" and "Richard", and they claimed that they were both New York City police officers. The two men told Budd Hopkins that they had been driving around the lower east side, when their vehicle suddenly stalled and came to a stop. They claim to have stalled just underneath the FDR Drive underpass. According to the story, the two witnesses told Mr. Hopkins, that while they were both standing outside of their car trying to identify the problem that had caused it to stall, they noticed a massive, disc-shaped flying object. It was hovering over an apartment building just across from the Brooklyn Bridge.

Already shocked by what they were seeing, they were even more startled when they saw a woman floating through the air. They said she was in an upright position as though standing and was being flanked by three unknown beings who were also floating upright through the air.

They claimed that the woman and her three alien escorts floated toward the giant, hovering disc shaped craft, and as they approached it, some kind of door opened and the woman and the trio of beings were allowed entry into the vessel. Once the floating women and the aliens were inside, the doorway closed behind them. The disc shaped craft reportedly then began to descend at an alarming rate and plunged into the East River, allegedly very close to Pier 17.

So with these two witnesses coming forward, it seemed that Linda's story had been validated and confirmed. But, as it would turn out, not only were these two men not being entirely sincere, but events were about to become truly terrifying for Linda Cortile.

Bizarre Twists and Secret Identities

It certainly must have been gratifying for Linda Cortile and Budd Hopkins to have had two witnesses come forward to corroborate Linda's story, however, things would soon take a very strange and sinister turn.

On a sunny day during the latter part of April in 1991, nearly a year and a half after the fateful night of Linda's UFO abduction, Linda was casually walking along a busy New York sidewalk minding her own business, when she suddenly found herself being abducted for a second time. However, this time she was not abducted by alien beings from another world; this time was snatched up by two very human men in a much more traditional, though no less frightening, abduction. In broad daylight and in front of a crowd of onlookers, these two men quite literally dragged a terrified screaming Linda into a waiting vehicle and drove off with her.

No less stunning than the kidnapping itself were the identities of the two perpetrators. The two men responsible for the second abduction of Linda Cortile were none other than the witnesses of the first, the supposed police officers known only as Dan and Richard.

As it turns out, Dan and Richard were not at all what they seemed. They were not police officers, as they had originally claimed, but rather they were in fact 'bodyguards'. On the night of Linda's alien abduction, Dan and Richard had been tasked with protecting the person of a rather unusual and unexpected individual: a high-ranking UN official by the name of Javier Perez de Cuellar. The car that had allegedly stalled across from the Brooklyn Bridge on the night of Linda's abduction was in fact this future UN Secretary General's limousine. It has been heavily suggested, although never confirmed on the record, that the UN official was also a witness to Linda's alien abduction that night in November 1989.

According to later testimony, after having witnessed the alien abduction, the two bodyguards were deeply emotionally and psychologically affected by the experience and had begun to act very strangely in the months following the event. Sources familiar with the men have since claimed that both of them, especially Dan, had become increasingly obsessed with Linda, allegedly to the point of stalking. Dan had supposedly become convinced that Linda had some kind of supernatural ability or that she was somehow able to exert her will and influence over people. Eventually their erratic thoughts and paranoid behavior reached a fever pitch, prompting the men to kidnap and interrogate Linda.

Dan and Richard held Linda captive and relentlessly interrogated her for many hours. During this interrogation, they made bizarre and seemingly paranoid accusations that Linda was somehow involved in strange events that had recently been occurring to Dan and Richard.

It has been said that during this extra-judicial detention and interrogation, Dan took on the role of the 'bad cop', pressing Linda for information, being aggressive, pushy and at times even violent with his captive. He refused to believe anything Linda would say in defense of herself. She tried to deny that she was somehow involved with orchestrating the alien abduction, but Dan just simply would not have it. He just kept getting more and more upset, erratic and irrational every time Linda attempted to make any protest.

Thankfully though, the men released Linda after a long and tense few hours. But this broad-daylight abduction, combined with the previous alien abduction, caused Linda a great deal of stress and anxiety, and unfortunately, Linda's traumatic ordeal would not end there.

About six months later, Linda was abducted a third time. This time, it was once again a human abduction, and again she was submitted to horrible and demeaning treatment. This time, however, it was not the pair of strange and suspicious men that took her, but rather, just the one known as Dan. He once again captured Linda and brought her to a hidden location somewhere on Long Island that Dan referred to as a 'safe house'. As though her kidnapping and poor treatment wasn't already demeaning enough for Linda, Dan allegedly forced Linda to put on a night gown, one that was very similar to the one that she had been wearing on the night of her alien abduction. It is unclear whether Dan was trying to recreate the night in question, or whether he felt that he could somehow glean some kind of new information by having Linda dress up in similar clothing to the night of her close encounter.

Linda did not see Richard anywhere in the safe house and it appeared that this abduction had been planned and perpetrated by Dan alone. Linda did however later claim that she remembered seeing CIA paperwork scattered about the safe house. This detail has led to further speculation as to the true nature of the occupation of this so-called 'Dan' and by extension his alleged partner 'Richard'. Had the two men been working on behalf of the CIA the entire time? If so, what interest would the CIA have in Linda Cortile's UFO/Alien encounter and abduction? While many witnesses have since come forward and even more clues have been analyzed, the real truth about just who exactly Dan and Richard were continues to elude us to this day.

In any event, Linda was able to break free and escape from her captor. However, following her escape, Linda led Dan on a foot chase that ended when he caught up with her and restrained her on a beach. Dan is said to have almost drowned Linda as he repeatedly began aggresively dunking her head into the ocean, whilst demanding explanations and answers to questions that Linda was simply unable to provide.

Fortunately, Linda was saved from this literal torture by none other than Richard. Richard suddenly appeared on the scene and convinced Dan that it would be in his best interest to release Linda. Dan relented and agreed to let Linda go. At that point, Richard brought a very traumatized Linda back to her home.

About a month later, Linda was surprised to find Richard showing up at her home unannounced. He told Linda that Dan's behavior had continued to become more and more unhinged and erratic and that his obsession over Linda had not relented. Richard claimed that Dan had, in fact, become so consumed by his obsession and his behavior had become so irrational that he had been committed to a mental health facility.

Further Witnesses and Inquiry

Around the same time all of these awful events were unfolding for Linda, Budd Hopkins received a letter from a woman who claimed to have also witnessed Linda Cortile's UFO abduction. The woman identified herself as Janet Trimble. On the night of Linda's initial abduction, Janet claimed that she had been driving her car along the Brooklyn Bridge, when she witnessed the UFO as the abduction was taking place. At the time, Mrs. Trimble had assumed that the bizarre scene she was witnessing in the Manhattan skyline must have been a film shoot for some kind of science fiction movie or something along those lines; it wasn't until some time later that Janet, in hindsight, began to suspect that she may have in fact witnessed something truly extraordinary.

Janet Trimble's eyewitness account corroborated many key details of the abduction story, both from Linda's perspective and that of Dan and Richard. With the official, documented account of a fourth witness, Budd Hopkins felt comfortable going public with new details of the Linda Cortile abduction that had been previously unknown to the media, and Linda herself also chose to share various new details of her story with publications.

With renewed media attention, a few additional witnesses also came forward. However, there was still a major setback for the investigation. That major setback, was the confirmation of the abduction story by the alleged key eyewitness, the UN Secretary General, Javier Perez de Cuellar. Mr. Cuellar never spoke publicly about the incident, and he has never confirmed or corroborated the story. However, Budd Hopkins did claim to have corresponded in great detail with Mr. Cuellar, and it is said that Mr. Cuellar did privately confirm details of the abduction with Mr. Hopkins.

Budd Hopkins was sure that Mr. Cuellar's testimony would be the smoking gun that the story needed to really make waves and become a massive and credible account of alien abduction. But sadly, for fear of career reprisals and loss of credibility, Mr. Cuellar has still to this day, refused to go public with his account of what he witnessed on that November night in 1989.

As such, Mr. Cuellar allegedly told Budd Hopkins, that if Budd ever went public with Mr Cuellar's involvment in the event, or if his association with the story ever became public knowledge by any other means, he would categorically deny it. This was of course very upsetting and frustrating for Budd Hopkins, but at the same time, he understood the position Mr. Cuellar was in.

As it stands, with Budd Hopkins now unfortunately deceased, the continued silence on the part of Mr. Cuellar, and the unknown status of the so-called "Dan" and "Richard", we may never know the full truth of the Linda Cortile Abduction.

4

THE BETTY ANDREASSON ABDUCTION

The story of Betty Andreasson's experiences with extraterrestrials and abductions is one that spans several decades and draws upon a vast tapestry of bizarre and paranormal events. The decades-long experiences of Mrs. Andreasson serve as something of a keystone case in the research and investigation of UFOs and alien abductions, as her whole, twisting and turning story shares many similarities with other famous UFO encounters and abduction stories, and simply by the fact her massive story has so much information to draw upon.

And while the abduction experiences of Mrs. Andreasson date all the way back to the mid-1940s, it was a particular event that took place in the winter of 1967 that set in motion the events that would lead to the full revelation of Betty Andreasson's extensive alien experiences.

One Winter Night in 1967

It was the evening of January the 25th, 1967. Betty Andreasson was in her home in South Ashburnham, Massachusetts with her parents and seven children. Her husband had recently been involved in a car crash and was still in the local hospital recovering from his injuries.

Despite the fact that they were in the middle of a late January Massachusetts winter, it was an unseasonably warm evening, and the snow was beginning to melt; which resulted in the entire area around the Andreasson's home being covered in a thick blanket of fog.

Sometime around 6:30 in the evening, and with no warning at all, every light in the entire house began to flicker. Everyone in the house stopped what they were doing and took notice of the unusual electrical disturbance. The flickering of household lights ended with a complete power failure that plunged the whole house — and the entire area — into total darkness. The family barely had time to react to this power blackout, however. Just a few seconds after the darkness took hold of the house, a strange glow began to creep through all of the windows into the house from outside. The light gradually turned into a bright, warm orange glow that lit up the entire inside of the house. Betty also later described this experience as though time were suddenly standing still and that it felt like she and her family were in some kind of vacuum.

She told her children to go into the living room and wait for her and their grandfather. In the kitchen, Betty and her father tried to figure out what was happening. Betty's father looked out of a kitchen window and was startled by what he saw; He claimed that he saw that the glowing light had completely bathed the area outside the house and that several figures, that he described as humanoid creatures, emerged from this bizarre light and began to approach the house.

As Betty's father attempted to tell Betty what he was seeing, one of the humanoid creatures suddenly appeared directly outside the kitchen window, in the exact spot where Betty's father happened to be looking. The creature turned toward the window, and the moment this alien being made eye contact with Betty's father, the man seemed to go into a bizarre state of trance, which Betty described as something like 'suspended animation'. He later claimed to have retained no memories of any of the events that took place after entering his paralyzed state of 'suspended animation'.

According to Betty, five of these humanoid alien beings somehow suddenly 'phased through the walls', as described by Betty, and were now inside the Andreasson's house. She said that the only way to describe the way the alien beings passed through the walls of the house was, as though they were fading in and out of existence.

Before long, all of Betty's children were placed under the same trance-like state as their grandfather and Betty was now the only person in the entire house who continued to be cognizant of her surroundings. The alien beings then requested that Betty come outside with them. She felt that it would be wise to do as they said, but at the same time, she was extremely concerned for her family's wellbeing and so she asked for some kind of assurance of their safety.

To alleviate Betty of her concerns for her family's safety, the beings released one of the children, a daughter named Becky, from her state of suspended animation. She was unharmed, and although at the time she retained no memory of the incident, it is important to note that years later, Becky was able to remember and corroborate the events of that fateful evening after undergoing hypnotic regression therapy.

With the proof that her family was safe, Betty agreed to follow the alien beings outside.

On Board an Alien Craft

While Betty Andreasson consciously followed the alien creatures under her own free will, she later described that she was floating through the air and that she also felt as though she was somehow being compelled to follow the alien beings.

Five of these strange alien creatures had phased through the walls into the house, but Betty only followed four of them back outside; One of the alien beings stayed behind in the house to guard the rest of the family members.

In the same manner the alien beings had somehow passed through the walls of the house, Betty too found herself performing the same supernatural feat. According to Betty, she simply floated through the wall as though it wasn't there. She had no idea how she was able to do this remarkable, unnatural feat, as she claimed that she was simply following the alien beings.

She said that she followed the beings outside and toward what she determined must have been the alien beings spacecraft. Betty described the vessel as being oval-shaped and featureless. After Betty followed the Alien beings into the other-worldy craft, she attempted to take stock of her new and bizarre surroundings; However, before she was able to fully examine the details around her, she said that she felt a sudden lurching sensation in the alien craft. She realized what she was feeling; It was the craft lifting off the ground and raising upward into the air at what must have been an extraordinary speed.

Betty said that she was submitted to a whole host of various examinations and procedures whilst onboard the alien craft. After an unknown amount of time spent undergoing these examinations, Betty claims that she was placed inside some kind of tank that was filled with an unknown liquid. She was also made to consume some other kind of strange liquid and she described it to have something of a tranquilizing effect upon her. She also recalls hearing an entire chorus of alien voices, all telling her that they had something important that they wanted to show to the world and that they had chosen her to do so on their behalf.

Betty claims that she suddenly found herself back inside her house. She did not recall how she got there or how long she had been aboard the alien craft. The alien humanoids were still with her in the house, according to Betty, they were gently placing all of the Andreasson children into their beds. All of them appeared to still be in the trance-like states that the humanoid alien creatures had earlier placed them in, along with Betty's father, who was also being put to bed by the alien beings.

As Betty watched this all take place before her, she recalls that one of the alien beings told her that it was the intention of the alien beings to help humanity and that they only had good and positive intentions. The alien being explained that, as a species, they were hesitant to reveal themselves to humanity, as they felt that in all likelihood, humans would fear the aliens and would have a difficult time accepting them.

She also added that she had been told by the alien beings, that they were not bound by time in the same way that human beings are. But the most shocking and potentially amazing thing that these strange alien creatures told Betty, was that the human body is not simply made of mere flesh and blood.

Unfortunately, according to Betty Andreasson, the aliens did not elaborate on the meaning of the assertion that our bodies are more than flesh and blood. Could these alien beings have been suggesting that humans do indeed possess spiritual souls? Perhaps it is unwise for this author to make any kind of personal interpretation as to the meaning of 'more than flesh and blood'.

Investigation

Despite the fact that Betty Andreasson was the only member of the entire family to have been taken aboard the alien craft and the only member of the family to have been conscious during the entire close encounter event, she did not immediately remember all of the details of the evening. While she did retain glimpses of some of the aspects of her ordeal, she could not recall all of the events of her experience in full detail; at least not until approximately one whole decade later.

In the immediate aftermath of the abduction incident, Betty Andreasson and her family were left in the same state of extreme confusion that so many alien abductees are often saddled with after experiencing a close encounter of the fourth kind. While the rest of the Andreasson family did not immediately recall anything at all about the evening of the abduction, and Betty Andreasson could only recall vague images, over time the whole family gradually began to remember the events of the close encounter.

It was as though some kind of memory block had been placed into the minds of the Andreasson family, and it was slowly but surely wearing off. With time, all of their memories of that unusually warm winter evening in 1967 came back in full; All of them except for Betty, as her memory of the incident was still fragmented.

Eventually in 1977, a full decade after the incident, Betty Andreasson contacted local UFO researchers who were actively seeking alien abductees for research purposes. At first, the researchers did not respond to Betty Andreasson's correspondence, as they felt that her story was far too fantastical to possibly be true. They concluded that she must have made up the story for attention, or perhaps even for financial gain. But Betty persisted, and she continued to insist upon the veracity of her story to the researchers.

Eventually, the UFO researchers requested that Betty take a polygraph test. They felt that such a test would be suitable enough to prove that she was lying about her abduction claims and they would be able to send her on her way and would never to be bothered by her ever again. However, much to the shock and surprise of the UFO researchers, Betty passed the lie detector test with flying colors.

Suddenly, and unsurprisingly, the UFO researchers were much more interested in Betty's fantastical alien abduction story. The UFO researchers put Betty in contact with one, Dr. Raymond Fowler. It was by working with Dr. Fowler over the course of a year, that Betty was able to finally able remember the full details of her abduction. Previously, the only memories to have come back on their own, where that of the orange light in the kitchen and the five alien beings phasing through the wall of her kitchen. Now, with her memories fully restored, she was able to bring much more credence to the story and allowed for more details to be corroborated.

During the initial investigation, several details of Betty's story were able to be corroborated in order to further validate her account. For example, hospital records show that Betty's husband had indeed been admitted to hospital for the period between mid-January through to March of 1967. This explained why Betty's parents had been staying with the family and validated that piece of circumstantial evidence.

Moreover, one very specific detail that Betty and the rest of the family recalled was that it was a relatively warm evening, and despite the warmth, there was still snow on the ground and there was also a thick covering of fog. This detail is verified by the weather records for the area; the weather records showed that it was indeed unseasonably warm for the time of year and the warmth had been causing the snow to melt. These weather conditions led to the very heavy fog that was experienced — and now corroborated — by Betty and the family.

Also of note, was the power outage that occurred in the moments before the strange orange light began to illuminate the Andreasson home. Regional records and local accounts all verify that there was indeed a power outage in the area at the exact moment that Betty claims the lights went out in the Andreasson home.

But while these corroborations of various pieces of circumstantial evidence must have been validating for the Andreasson family, it by no means was the end of the story. No, in fact, Betty was about to find out that her experience on the night of January 25th, 1967, wasn't even the first time that she had been abducted by aliens.

Decades of Abductions

Through hypnotic regression therapy, Betty Andreasson and Dr. Fowler were able to uncover a whole plethora of events and experiences from Betty's earlier life that had been blocked from her memories, either by means of some sort of alien technology or Betty's own psychological defense mechanisms. And although it's unclear by what means these memories were blocked, once Betty's memories were recovered they revealed all manner of experiences that would have a major effect on Betty Andreasson's life, not to mention major implications as to what the alien creatures intentions were with her.

From what Dr. Fowler and Betty Andreasson were able to discern based on Betty's accounts under regression, her first abduction experience happened back in the year 1944. Betty was no more than seven years old at the time. Under regression, she recalled that she had been waiting in a play house for a friend to arrive, when she suddenly saw a strange red-colored orb float into the small interior of the play house. She recounted that the orb floated up to her and stopped right in in front of her eyes. As this occurred, she began to hear voices inside her head. They told her that they would be watching her, and that they would see her again when she was twelve years old.

This promise would indeed come true, as revealed by Betty's regressions. Some five years later, in the year 1949, a young, twelve-year-old Betty Andreasson, had been walking around a wooded area in the nearby region of Westminster, when she was suddenly approached by a grey creature that was wearing some kind of coverall outfit that was covered in symbols. The grey alien being pressed a button that was located on it's outfit and a floating red orb appeared. Again, as had happened five years earlier in the playhouse, the red orb floated toward her and settled directly in front of her eyes. Once again, she heard voices in her head.

Just one year later, in the year 1950, the now thirteen-year-

Old Betty Andreasson would be not just receive a visit from the alien beings, but for the first time, she was abducted by the strange creatures as well. She was lead aboard an alien craft by a strange orb-like object. Once she was on board, a bizarre alien instrument was placed on the inside of her mouth. Betty recalled that the device seemed to hold down her tongue, but she could not divine any other purpose for it. She was shown a large wheel of sorts that was made of some kind of rubber. She said that the Alien craft that she was travelling in plunged into a body of water. The young Betty did not know what body of water it was, but the craft would later emerge within some kind of underground base. Betty later recalled being led though a curious place that she described as a 'museum of time'. This 'museum' had on display what seemed to be human beings from all cultures and periods of time throughout history. These human beings were being held in what appeared to be some kind of casing made of glass.

In this author's opinion, it is somewhat unsettling to imagine this 'museum' filled with people on display from various time periods and cultures. During the 1967 abduction of Betty, these alien beings told Betty that they only had good intentions and that they wanted to help humanity. But one has to question if the motivation of these alien beings is truly one of benevolence when they are willing to steal people away from their loved ones and keep them forever encased within glass in some underground 'museum of time'. In this author's personal opinion, this would be an act of cruelty, not benevolence. How many people have these aliens kidnapped over the many millennia to be put on display in this 'museum of time'? How much heartbreak and pain have these alien beings caused for the many friends and family members of people who have been taken and never returned?

Betty Andreasson was a very devoutly religious person for her entire life. This likely had a deep impact on the way she perceived these abduction experiences. On many occasions, she referred to these alien beings as 'angels'. Whether Betty's angelic assessment of the alien entities is simply a way for her to rationalize the existence of these alien beings in a way that is familiar to her religious understanding, or if there some truth in her interpretation is anybody's guess; But unfortunately, Betty's belief in a religious explanation for her abductions and visitation experiences has led many to discredit Betty Andreasson's story.

In any event, the story of the abduction of Betty Andreasson and the entire Andreasson family, is a story with many intriguing details. It is a story that gives us many clues as to the nature of the unknown alien beings that contact us, and what their true intentions may or may not be.

5

THE KELLY CAHILL ENCOUNTER

Accounts of extra-terrestrials and UFO's fall broadly under the umbrella of the 'paranormal' for many people. Of course, many alien abduction stories do not include any paranormal elements at all and would perhaps be more appropriately associated with science and technology. The story of Kelly Cahill and her close encounter with alien beings is definitely one with more than a whiff of the paranormal about it. Her close encounter story shares many similarities with a truly terrifying paranormal phenomenon: the shadow people.

An Unforgettable Encounter

Just after midnight, in the first few minutes of the 8th of august in 1993, twenty-seven-year-old Kelly Cahill was driving through the foothills in the Mount Dandenong region of Victoria, Australia with her husband.

As the family car made its way around a bend in the road, they came across something that would change their lives forever. Right in the middle of the road, hovering just a few feet in the air was a large, disc-shaped object. A dazzling array of bright, colorful lights adorned the underside of the disc. This disc-shaped craft had windows that were clearly visible from the Cahill's vantage point, and through these windows the Cahill's could see dark, shadowy beings that were presumably controlling this disc-shaped vessel.

Kelly recalls screaming, completely involuntarily. She wanted to ask her husband if he was seeing the same thing that she was seeing, but the moment she tried to speak, the disc-shaped craft seemed to abruptly vanish in an instant.

However, when Kelly and her husband looked up into the sky, they were able to see a bright light. Immediately after locating the object glowing in the sky, the light started to become brighter and brighter, to the point that it was painful to keep staring at it.

The Immediate Aftermath

Just a mere moment after witnessing the disc-shaped craft and being exposed to the blinding bright light, Kelly recalls that the bright light was suddenly gone and they were traveling along the road once again with her husband in control of the vehicle. Kelly felt extremely confused. She asked her husband if she had blacked out. Kelly's husband did not know whether or not Kelly had lost consciousness, but unbeknownst to Kelly at the time, Kelly's husband was also wondering the same thing about himself.

What had happened? One moment, they were seeing a massive disc-shaped craft and a blinding light in the sky, and the next moment, the craft and the light were gone without a trace and the couple were driving along the road again, as though nothing out of the ordinary had happened.

Shaken by the experience, both Kelly and her husband found themselves unable to discuss the bizarre incident, or anything else, for the rest of the drive home. They were both keenly aware that they had just experienced something truly extraordinary.

When they arrived home, the couple were surprised to discover that the drive had taken an hour longer than it should have. Somehow, they had lost an entire hour during their drive home and they had no memory of what had happened within that lost hour.

As Kelly prepared to go to bed that evening, she noticed that she had a bizarre triangular mark on her torso that hadn't been there previously.

For the next two weeks following that strange evening, Kelly experienced a host of health problems and general illness. She found herself admitted to the hospital twice, the first time was in response to a particularly aggressive infection, and the second was on account of serious stomach pains.

In the weeks that followed, flashes of memory began to work their way into Kelly's conscious mind and she was able to begin to piece back together the events of the close encounter. Once her memories of the event came back in full, it would come to be one of the strangest and interesting close encounter accounts that we have on record.

Old Memories and New Witnesses

As Kelly's memories began to return, they revealed events that were notably different from how she and her husband had initially remembered them. She came to recall that the disc-shaped craft that they had come upon in the middle of the road, had in fact been initially in a ditch off to the side of the road. Kelly's husband had stopped the car upon seeing this otherworldly craft. Of particular note, while Kelly's initial memories took place entirely within the Cahill's vehicle, these newly recovered memories indicated that Kelly and her husband had both exited the car in order to get a better look at the highly unusual craft in the ditch on side of the road.

Kelly recalled, that whilst she and her husband were outside observing the disc-shaped craft, another car came down the road. This other car initially appeared as though it would pass by the strange scene, but instead it came to a stop just beside the Cahill's car. No doubt, the occupants of this second car had stopped for some reason the Cahill's had, to take a look the strange disc-shaped craft.

Kelly remembered that the alien craft seemed to possesses what she described as some type of 'magnetic force', that was pulling her and her husband in. She said that it was as though she and her husband found themselves moving toward the craft against their conscious will. Whether this was due to some kind of actual 'magnetic' technology or some trick of the mind that drew them toward the disc-shaped craft is unclear.

As Kelly got closer to the craft, she saw what appeared to be some kind of alien being. It appeared to have a humanoid shape and was about the height of a very tall adult human, but this being was certainly no human. The alien being was a deep black in color, but this blackness was not due to it having a dark skin tone. No, this was a blackness, unlike anything Kelly had ever seen before. This being wasn't just dark in color, it was, as Kelly later put it, completely devoid of color. Blacker than black. She described feeling a sense that this dark being had no soul. She said that it was approximately seven feet tall and that it was almost unnaturally thin.

Another aspect of the dark being's appearance that Kelly found to be deeply unsettling, was its eyes. Kelly described the being as having piercing eyes that glowed a deep and ominous red. She claimed that these red eyes were overly large and strangely out of proportion with the bizarre dark being's head.

When a fearful Kelly looked away from this dark being, she realized that there were several more of the frightening creatures. In the blink of an eye, an entire group of the beings appeared immediately in front of Kelly and her husband. She described the speed at which they moved to be startling and entirely unnatural. Despite the extreme fright of being intercepted by a group of terrifying and potentially dangerous dark beings, Kelly still had enough of her wits to notice that a second group of the dark beings had moved with the same unnatural speed to confront and surround the the other car that had stopped nearby.

The absolute terror gripping Kelly was too much and she was unable to handle it anymore. As the dark beings reached out with their long fingered dark hands to take hold of Kelly and her husband, Kelly screamed.

The next thing Kelly knew, she was suddenly back in her car with her husband traveling home. Any memories that she may have had of the time between being confronted by the terrifying dark alien creatures and being back in her car with her husband were seemingly gone.

Alien Life Forms or Shadow People?

Kelly Cahill was at first very hesitant to talk publicly about her and her husband's terrifying close encounter. She strongly felt that no one would possibly believe their wild story about encountering an alien craft and strange, frightening, soulless black shadow beings. Apart from her and her husband's own eyewitness accounts, there was no real way to corroborate their story. Except of course for the people that had been in the second car, they were the only other witnesses to the whole strange event.

And sure enough, the people in the second car, another married couple with a friend, did come forward and gave their accounts of the events from that night. Their story would corroborate Kelly Cahill's version of events, in fact, it was point for point exactly how Kelly remembered the frightening event unfolding. If nothing else, this convinced Kelly and her husband that they had, in fact, experienced these events and that they were not simply false memories or something that they imagined.

In the days and weeks following that fateful evening, Kelly experienced reoccurring nightmares. These nightmares were extremely intense and frequently involved a frightening being staring down upon her in her bed, that she described as a 'black alien'. Intriguingly, this shadowy black alien being seemed to be particularly interested in Kelly's torso. In fact, in all of these nightmares, the dark being seemed to be peering rather intently at the exact spot where she had discovered the strange triangular marking on her body.

This unsettling element to the Kelly's story has led many an investigator to believe that what Kelly experienced was not an alien abduction at all, but rather an encounter with the paranormal entities commonly known as 'shadow people'.

The phenomenon of shadow people is not a new one. There have been innumerable worldwide reports of people who have witnessed these paranormal entities. Often, people first report seeing a shadow person in the corner of their eye, usually just as a fleeting glimpse. People often tend to dismiss these fleeting glimpses of shadow people as a trick of the light, or simply their imagination running wild. Yet, shadow people are much, much more than that; they are truly one of the most terrifying entities in the entire paranormal spectrum.

Many encounters with shadow people result in the witnesses being deeply emotionally affected by the experience for many days, weeks, and in some cases, years after the encounter. Shadow people are thought to mostly visit people at night when they are in bed and are often associated with a condition known as sleep paralysis. It is not entirely clear whether or not the shadow people themselves are the cause of sleep paralysis, or if they are simply a psychological hallucination caused by the sleep paralysis condition itself, though there are many theories to support both arguments.

No one truly knows for certain what intentions the shadow people may have, or what purposes they serve. What we do know, is that they nearly always share the same appearance; A tall, humanoid figure that is completely void of all light and color. Their appearance has been described as being like a human-shaped hole in the fabric of the universe, and they are said to be darker than the dark of night. Shadow people are said to have a presence about them that witnesses often describe as being pure evil, and witnesses often feel a deep sense of dread when seeing a shadow person. While not always the case, witnesses to shadow people will sometimes report seeing red eyes on said shadow person.

Truly a terrifying image, and one that is highly consistent with the beings that were allegedly witnessed by Kelly Cahill, her husband, and the occupants of the second car that extraordinary night.

The phenomenon of shadow people is far more often associated with the paranormal than it is with UFO encounters, and yet, it's hard to dismiss the similarities between witness accounts of shadow people and the dark beings encountered in Kelly Cahill and her husband. Is it possible that this may have been a case of mis-identification, or are we dealing with a new type of alien encounter? Ever since this story made its way into the public consciousness and into the awareness of UFO researchers and enthusiasts, many more people have come forward claiming that their close encounter experiences were followed by frequent and in some cases prolonged visitations by beings that share many, many similarities with the strange entities described as shadow people.

Could there be more going on here than meets the eye? When one considers the unimaginable vastness of space, the mind boggles. The distances between star systems is so great, that the idea of alien beings making the journey from some distant planet to ours, is a concept that is little bit hard for some people to swallow. Of course, it's certainly within the realm of possibility that alien beings simply possess technology that is far more advanced than ours, and this highly advanced technology could mean that the vast distances of space do not present the same kind of prohibitive challenge as it would for us. But given the vastness of space, is it perhaps possible that some, if not all, alien beings that have been encountered over the years by thousands of people worldwide, could in fact be inter-dimensional visitors to our world rather than visitors from another planet? Is it possible that the dark shadow beings encountered by Kelly Cahill and her husband were inter-dimensional beings rather than extra-terrestrial ones? Could all alien beings be from a different plane of space-time altogether? When one recalls, that during the Betty Andreasson abduction, the alien beings told Betty Andreasson that they were not bound by time in the same manner that humans are; does that then suggest that they may come from a different plane of reality outside of time itself?

If all close encounters with alien beings, UFO's and the seemingly paranormal phenomenon of shadow people are in indeed somehow interrelated, then why was the Cahill's close encounter so terrfyingly different from encounters with seemingly kind alien beings, like those encountered by the Longley family or the Andreassons? Is it simply due to the grey aliens encountered by Longleys and Andreassons being of a different species to the dark shadow aliens encountered by the Cahills? Or could there be a much deeper, complicated and perhaps even spiritual explanation for the differences? Betty Andreasson's deeply religious upbringing has led her to believe that the alien beings that she has encountered throughout her life are in fact angels. However, the dark shadowy entities encountered by Kelly Cahill and her husband seem to be the exact polar opposite of the friendly aliens encountered by the Longley Family and Betty Andreasson, indeed, the dark shadow beings encountered by the Cahills seemed to have an almost demonic presence to them. It almost makes one wonder, if perhaps the stories of religious encounters with angels and demons throughout history have in fact been encounters with these various strange, and polar opposite in nature, alien beings.

Deeper Connections and Darker Implications

The strange close encounter that Kelly Cahill and her husband experienced happened over twenty-five years ago and many mysteries still abound in regard her story. Yet, slowly, some of these mysteries seem as though they may be coming to light.

In February of the year 2017, a number of CIA documents were declassified regarding the spy agency's research and experiments into 'remote viewing'. (Remote viewing is the practice of seeking impressions about a distant or unseen target, through use of extrasensory perception or "sensing" with the mind via psychic means) While much of the information contained in these declassified documents is new to researchers, knowledge of CIA experiments into remote viewing is far from new. Many UFO and paranormal researchers have been deeply familiar with the CIA's experiments into remote viewing for many, many years. However, some of the details that were uncovered in these declassified documents are very interesting when compared to the accounts of Kelly Cahill and others with experiences involving shadow people.

One of these declassified documents, dated to the year 1984 (nearly a full decade before Kelly Cahill's close encounter), details the remotely viewed images of strange beings that were described by remote viewers as being very tall and thin shadowy people. But what is truly bizarre about these declassified accounts of remotely viewed beings, is not the nature of the beings themselves, but rather the location of where these dark beings had supposedly once been located. The remote viewer test subjects were given a set of coordinates to remotely view. However, these coordinates were not of a location found anywhere on Earth, rather, these coordinates were of the planetary location of our neighboring planet, Mars. More intriguingly though, these coordinates were not of where Mars had been presently located at that particular time in 1984, no, these were coordinates for where Mars would have been located one million years previous.

That's right, as unbelievable as it may sound, there exists official declassified CIA documents that report remote views of what appears to be shadow people, that were located on Mars one million years ago. It is reported within this declassified document, that the remote viewers witnessed a small group of these ancient shadow aliens leaving Mars, in order to find another home on another planet. Furthermore, the description that the remote viewers gave of the craft that these dark beings had purportedly used to leave Mars was strikingly similar to the description that Kelly Cahill gave of the craft that she and her husband had witnessed.

Could the beings encountered by Kelly Cahill and her husband, in fact, be ancient shadow people from Mars? Did the shadow beings, that were witnessed leaving mars one million years ago by CIA remote viewing test subjects, find their new home here on Earth? We may never know the answers to these questions, but nonetheless, they are certainly fascinating questions to ponder.

6

Conclusion

Thank you for making it through to the end of *Close Encounters Volume 2: The Abduction Cases of Charles Hickson & Calvin Parker, Scott & Wendy Longley, Linda Cortile, Betty Andreasson, and Kelly Cahill.* I hope that you enjoyed reading this book as much as I did writing it.

There is certainly no shortage of strange activity that takes place on this planet, not to mention, off this planet. The preceding five stories of alien abduction featured in this book only scratch the surface of the otherworldly activity that is taking place all around the world on a daily basis. If you wish to keep exploring the fascinating and mysterious topic of UFO's and alien abduction, there are countless books out there on topic, written by many different talented authors and experts on the subject. Keep researching this fascinating topic with care and passion, and you will continue to be exposed to a world which most people cut themselves off from, consciously or otherwise.

And of course, for more intriguing and mysterious true stories of UFO's and alien abduction, be sure to keep your

CONCLUSION

eyes peeled for future volumes of this 'Close Encounters' book series as well.

And remember… Watch the skies.